Laura Ingalls Wilder

Jennifer Strand

abdopublishing.com

Published by Abdo Zoom™, PO Box 398166, Minneapolis, Minnesota 55439. Copyright © 2017 by Abdo Consulting Group, Inc. International copyrights reserved in all countries. No part of this book may be reproduced in any form without written permission from the publisher. Abdo Zoom™ is a trademark and logo of Abdo Consulting Group, Inc.

Printed in the United States of America, North Mankato, Minnesota
062016
092016

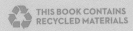
Cover Photo: Laura Ingalls Wilder Memorial Society, Inc.
Interior Photos: Laura Ingalls Wilder Memorial Society, De Smet, S.D., 1, 7, 10; Bettmann/Corbis, 5; iStockphoto, 6–7, 9, 10–11, 14–15; North Wind Picture Archives, 8; Brian A Jackson/iStockphoto, 12; South Dakota State Historical Society, 13; Shutterstock Images, 15; The Kucker Studio/National Archives-Herbert Hoover Presidential Library, 16; Mansfield Art Studio/National Archives-Herbert Hoover Presidential Library, 17; Schupp Studio/National Archives-Herbert Hoover Presidential Library, 18

Editor: Emily Temple
Series Designer: Madeline Berger
Art Direction: Dorothy Toth

Publisher's Cataloging-in-Publication Data
Names: Strand, Jennifer, author.
Title: Laura Ingalls Wilder / by Jennifer Strand.
Description: Minneapolis, MN : Abdo Zoom, [2017] | Series: Amazing authors |
    Includes bibliographical references and index.
Identifiers: LCCN 2016941362 | ISBN 9781680792157 (lib. bdg.) |
    ISBN 9781680793833 (ebook) | 9781680794724 (Read-to-me ebook)
Subjects: LCSH: Wilder, Laura Ingalls, 1867-1957--Juvenile literature. |
    American authors--20th century--Biography--Juvenile literature. | Frontier
    and pioneer life--United States--Juvenile literature. | Children's stories--
    Authorship--Juvenile literature. | Women authors--20th century--Biography--
    Juvenile literature. | Authorship--Juvenile literature. | Children's literature--
    Technique--Juvenile literature.
Classification: DDC 813/.52 [B]--dc23
LC record available at http://lccn.loc.gov/2016941362

Table of Contents

Introduction

Laura Ingalls Wilder was an author. She and her family were **pioneers**. Wilder wrote books about their lives.

5

Early Life

Laura was born in 1867.
She grew up on the frontier.
The family spent a lot
of time together.

Laura and her sisters were homeschooled.

Rise to Fame

The Ingalls family moved a lot.

They had to survive harsh weather.
They also farmed crops.

9

Laura Ingalls started teaching.
Then she met Almanzo Wilder.

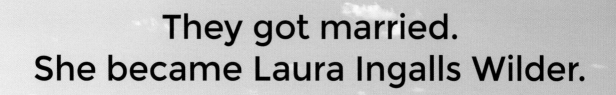

They got married.
She became Laura Ingalls Wilder.

Career

Wilder began
writing about her family.

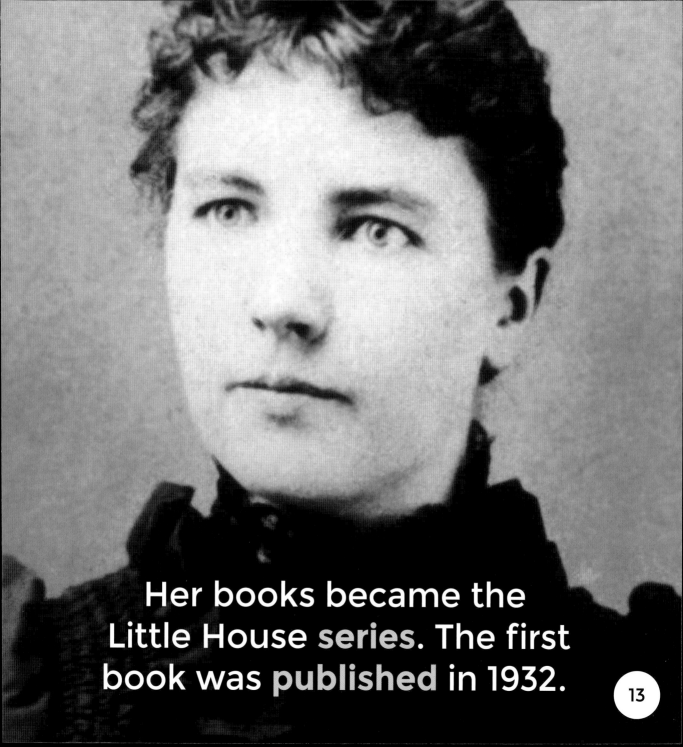

Her books became the Little House **series**. The first book was **published** in 1932.

The Little House books were filled with adventure.

They became **popular**.
People enjoyed the stories
of pioneer life.

Legacy

Wilder wrote eight books about her childhood.
She became famous.

But she continued to live
on her farm.

Wilder died in 1957. Her books are still popular today. They are a reminder of early American life.

Quick Stats

Laura Ingalls Wilder

Born: February 7, 1867

Birthplace: near Pepin, Wisconsin

Husband: Almanzo Wilder

Known For: Wilder wrote the popular Little House series of books.

Died: February 10, 1957

1867: Laura Elizabeth Ingalls is born on February 7.

1885: Laura Ingalls marries Almanzo Wilder on August 25.

1894: The Wilders move to Manfield, Missouri.

1932: The first Little House book is published.

1943: The last Little House book is published in Wilder's lifetime.

1957: Laura Ingalls Wilder dies on February 10.

Glossary

frontier - land where few people live.

harsh - unpleasant or difficult.

pioneers - people who do something that few have done before.

popular - liked by many people.

published - created so that others can access it.

series - a group of books or movies about the same characters.

Booklinks

For more information
on **Laura Ingalls Wilder**, please visit
booklinks.abdopublishing.com

Zoom In on Biographies!

Learn even more with the Abdo Zoom
Biographies database. Check out
abdozoom.com for more information.

Index